Po Panda's Great Adventure

By
Ramona Driscoll

Hello, I'm Po Panda, that's what they say, named after a panda in a playful way.

Do I look like a bear, you might ask? Well, my mama thinks it's quite the task! I love to explore, run, and play with my mama by my side, mostly on sunny days!

One morning bright, the world's in view, I meet a squirrel up in a tree so true. I barked, "Hello!" with a friendly tone, But the squirrel said, "Nuts, I must gather, alone." "No time to play," the squirrel did explain. So I continued my journey, free from disdain.

A bunny hops into my sight, I run to greet with all my might. But the bunny is fast, and away it hops, Mama says, "No, Po," and my excitement plops

Though my tail's still wagging, I can't resist the smells on the ground, they persist. A muddy puddle, oh, what delight, I stomp and splash, what a funny sight! Mama yells, "No," a bit too late. My white fur's brown, my playful fate.

Momma says we must go home for a bath and comb, but I don't like either of those. So, momma has to gently coax me home, where I protest with a little grumble.

We head back home, a bath in store, but I don't like it, I can't ignore. In the tub, I squirmed and splash, Water's clutches, I tried to dash. I leaped out onto mama's lap, so true. Now we're both wet, with giggles anew.

She chuckles as she dries me well, Warm and cozy,
you can tell. She combs my fur with love and care,
Hugs and scratches, I'm a happy Po Bear.

Off to bed, where dreams take flight, of friends I've met, in the day so bright. The chatty squirrel and playful bunny too, and that marvelous mud puddle, it's all true. But no matter how hard we may try, some friends won't always have time to comply. But it's okay, we can be patient and kind, Give them space, and respect, in our heart and mind.

Po Panda's adventures never end, with love from mama, and furry friends. Each day's a journey, a brand new start, filled with fun, surprises, and love from the heart.

www.ingramcontent.com/pod-product-compliance
Lightning Source LLC
Chambersburg PA
CBHW072009170726
47999CB00013B/1235